HEAVY METAL NURSING

Heavy Metal Nursing

POEMS

Scott Frey

UNIVERSITY OF TAMPA PRESS

Manufactured in the United States of America
First Edition

Cover photography by Liss Couch-Edwards

Cover design by Ana C. Alvarado Diaz

The University of Tampa Press
401 West Kennedy Boulevard
Tampa, FL 33606

ISBN 978-1-59732-210-2 (pbk.)
ISBN 978-1-59732-211-9 (hbk.)
ISBN 978-1-59732-212-6 (ebk.)

Library of Congress Cataloging-in-Publication Data

Names: Frey, Scott, author.
Title: Heavy metal nursing : poems / Scott Frey.
Other titles: Heavy metal nursing (Compilation)
Description: First edition. | Tampa, FL : University of Tampa Press, 2024.
| Summary: "Heavy Metal Nursing tells a story of love which, like all
love stories, is a story of loss. It is not a sentimental love but a
"heavy-metal" one, kneeling arm-to-arm beside parents caring for their
daughter born with a severe brain injury who needs intensive care her
entire life and dies at three years old. These poems hum the music of
oxygen machines and chest compressions and respond to suffering with
"half howl, half prayer." These are poems of vulnerability and pain, but
also of parenting, caregiving, marriage, medicine, humor, tenderness,
affection. Over and over, they ask what it means to be "learning / to
make life out of this slow dying.""-- Provided by publisher.
Identifiers: LCCN 2024017561 (print) | LCCN 2024017562 (ebook) | ISBN
9781597322102 (paperback ; acid-free paper) | ISBN 9781597322119
(hardback ; acid-free paper) | ISBN 9781597322126 (ebook)
Subjects: LCGFT: Poetry.
Classification: LCC PS3606.R4886 H43 2024 (print) | LCC PS3606.R4886
(ebook) | DDC 811/.6--dc23/eng/20240422
LC record available at https://lccn.loc.gov/2024017561
LC ebook record available at https://lccn.loc.gov/2024017562

Browse & order online at
http://www.utampapress.org

For all those who give good care to the end

and then continue, wielding what gifts they can

For Meryl, the realest metal worker

Always, for Charlotte

Contents

The Pumping Room | 1

1

She Exits the Womb as Though on a Gurney | 3
7 North (NICU, Children's Hospital Boston) | 4
Outside the Open Door of the Physician Assistant's Office | 6
Coming Home Without You | 7
Heavy Metal Nursing | 8
Prayer | 10
Thanksgivings | 12
Two Better People | 14
Velcro Ode | 16
Danvers State Mental Hospital | 18
Hypothermia Part 1 | 19
To the Vision Box | 20
Night Nurses | 22
After Two and a Half Years, Our Daughter Smiles | 23

2

Learning to See | 25
Encomium is an Anagram of Meconium | 26
Hypothermia Part 2 | 28
Assist | 30
Halloween Parade, Children's Hospital Boston | 32
Instructions for Deep Suction | 33
When the Conference Room Where We are to Plan Our Daughter's Death
Looks Like the Room Where We Learned of Her Brain Injury | 35

The Extraction Team | 36

Chucks | 38

The Blanket on the Bench | 40

My Sisters Paint My Dying Three-Year-Old's Nails | 41

The Morning After My Daughter's Death, Cleaning Out Her Med Cabinet | 42

Grief | 44

Lacing 'Em Up | 45

Pink Feather Boa | 46

3

West Beach | 50

Pass It On | 51

New Neighborhood | 52

Mustard Seeds | 56

In the Lobby | 57

Soul Stone | 58

Standing In It | 59

Breaking My Favorite Mug | 60

West Beach Again | 61

Fake Zombies | 62

To the Flour Handprints on My Wife's Pants | 64

A Difficult Stick | 67

I'm Writing a Tornado | 73

Sneezing | 74

Upon Hearing the Animals One Mile into a Long Day's Drive Back to My PA Hometown | 76

My Three-Year-Old Wears the Shirt Her Older Sister Wore the Day She Died at Three Years Old | 79

Notes | 81
Acknowledgements | 82
About the Author | 87
About the Book | 89

*"We never thought about how we might parent a child
for whom there is no future."*

—Emily Rapp Black, "Notes From a Dragon Mom"

*"The torch has sputtered
On its side in the rain
Light it again"*

—Edward Hirsch, Gabriel

The Pumping Room

Outside the noises and needs
of the neonatal ICU,
the hallway sign says, *Pumping Room.*
Could be a porn channel,
I whisper to my wife.
She mentions milk
and an udder, chuckles,
as we wheel a yellow *Symphony*
with its cord and coiled tubes.

I pull on the blue gloves
for a smaller nurse's hands,
massage my wife's knotted ducts
while she cups a plastic funnel
with each hand. My thumbs
and hairy wrists break through
thin latex like baby robins,
shredded gloves dangling
like old shells
as we coax forth milk
for the small, tender mouth
that might never drink it.
She fills the bottles and
I turn the *Symphony* off.
No matter how quickly
I remove the cups
and she replaces the pads,
thin jets arc into the air
washing us with sweet milk
as we crack up,
anointed anew
for the work set before us.

1

She Exits the Womb as Though on a Gurney

Where her first screams should be there is silence.
She exits the womb as though on a gurney,
Only the scissors' dull snip echoes in the room.
Blue gowns hover around her; still and pale

She exits the womb as though on a gurney:
Arms flexed tight, her pulse plunges and spikes.
Blue gowns swirling over her still and pale
In the infant warmer. A rift opens wide.

Arms flexed tight her pulse plunges and spikes.
My wife pleads, *Is she okay?* I lie, *She seems fine.*
In the infant warmer, a rift opens wide.
The walls become the damp packed sides of a grave.

I say *she seems fine* when my wife pleads *Is she okay?*
The silence swallows all our questions but one—
The walls become the slick sides of a grave.
In the conference room they hold up photos of her brain.

The silence swallows all our questions but one.
The nurse's stethoscope dangles like a noose.
In the conference room they hold up photos of her brain;
Visions of her skipping in the surf start to fade.

The nurse's stethoscope dangles like a noose.
Where her first screams should be: silence.
Visions of her skipping in the surf start to fade.
Only the scissors' dull snip echoes in the room.

7 North (NICU, Children's Hospital Boston)

For David & Babs Swanson

Take care of her, your wife whispers.
She pleads from her hospital bed
for your hours-old daughter whose body—
loaded with phenobarbital

to stay the seizures—is anchored
in a sea of white sheets on the gurney
as they lift her into the ambulance.
In Boston, you watch them wheel her

to an isthmus between bays
of breathing tubes and plastic wombs.
Forty hours it's been since this labor
began. And after they try and fail,

and after failing try and fail and try
again to find a vein, while they pull
the blue curtain to make a sterile room
for running a line into her

umbilical artery, they send you
to wait in a room whose walls
you can almost spread your arms
to touch, though opened wings

do not come to mind. Overhead
the Sox blur on TV. There you
lean—past bargaining, past pleading
or prayer—feeling the cool wall

that holds you upright. It's then
that a hand appears on your shoulder.
Its partner passes the plate:
Doritos and half a sandwich

he says he's not going to eat, then
offers a Styrofoam cup. Ginger ale.
Says, *You just got here, huh?* Says,
Take and eat. And it's hard to pinpoint

but something shifts with this hand
out of the wilderness. Even after
you learn the next day that what's broken
in your daughter cannot be mended,

you'll take chips and a cup and pass them
to the couple one bay over
while their son's behind the blue curtain
and they step for the first time

into the room before learning
to make life out of this slow dying.

Outside the Open Door of the Physician Assistant's Office

A small room between the NICU and the pumping room
my wife and I are exiting, looking for a garbage can

to toss used gloves. We hear, floating into the hallway,
the unmistakable cadence of the shift change.

We hear in their rundown of patients' numbers and conditions
the fatigue in their throats. A few steps from the door

we hear, *medical record number 6928103.*
Cold knowledge creeps up our necks:

they're about to discuss our daughter.
Hypoxic ischemic encephalopathy.

My wife's fingers vise my arm. They say,
Doesn't have the capacity to seize, a clinical sentence

for the EEG findings but the words perfect
for the brutal truth: her brain's so damaged

even a seizure would be a sign of progress.
So all three of them laugh.

My wife jabs her finger towards the door. I step to it,
a voice in me urging *don't forget the tenderness*

of some of her nurses; don't get thrown out of the hospital.

Coming Home Without You

Inside the door
daisies loll in vases
on the counter. Tulips slump in
glass vessels by the base

of the glider assembled to
nurse and hold you. Tethered
there: *Welcome Home* and *It's a Girl*
balloons as your mother

collapses into it. While
her hands start to quiver
I crawl toward her knees, weeping
through the field of severed

flowers. On your new stitched blanket
ducks float in an empty sea.
She pulls it to her lap,
the place where you should be.

Heavy Metal Nursing

For months the small seizures we don't know are seizures
jolt our daughter awake
every ten minutes, day and night.
Our daughter's neurologist avoids our eyes
as he describes the damage.

The dirt from her first home nurse's boots
looks like Oreo crumbs on our beige carpet,
Like the soil is rich and good.
He wears a Metallica t-shirt and a sagging pair of jeans.
When our daughter sprays a mustard-colored blast on the wall
during a diaper change, he cries, *Whoops-a-daisy!*

He tells of a son named Andrew—after him.
I say *that's my brother's name.*
He calls his hometown *San Antone,*
tells how his Mexican parents hated his Sepultura t-shirt.
He's a single dad. Plays drums in a thrash band. Drives a gray Mustang
with an answer ready for the cops who always pull him over.
These are three reasons he often arrives late.
We tell him we didn't picture our daughter's nurse as a heavy metal drummer
with a labret piercing.
He says, *No one does.*

He is our daughter's nurse. That makes him a nurse for all of us.
When he plays guitar licks from "Sanitarium,"
they sound like what's roiling inside me.
When he eats his turkey sub for lunch, I sit down beside him.
When he brings his face low and close to our daughter's,
hunches his broad shoulders like he's leaning over his drums
and scoops her into his large hands,
he sings softly in her ear.

Bobbing his head to *Death Magnetic*, he's pulled over again.
Drifting on the yellow line the latest reason.
They're going to suspend my license, he tells us.
We see him drifting. Thinking of his kid in foster care.
Forgets to wash his hands. Extra cigarette breaks.
He sketches a tattoo for my back, the entrance to a labyrinth.
No faun or flute for guidance,
only a path winding into darkness.
When we need him,
he doesn't answer the phone.
Voicemail full.

Prayer

Her cries knife the fog
I stumble beneath

a duvet of drunken
sleep towards her crib.

My soul's deep plea
an emergency cord

to heaven, snatched
from my mouth by

a great wind. As I utter it
she wails again.

I reach out to end it,
to close my fist on her throat

instead palming her forehead
it sears my hand

I fumble through the basket
beside the changing table—

no thermometer—as her face
purples with screaming.

I rush to cool her turn
the shower cold as it will go

step between its frosted panes
into the bitter blast of water

which could cause the seizure
we're trying to avoid

her shrieks tear the ceiling
in pieces on top of us

droplets streaking
the shower panels

like my prayers down
God's closed window

Thanksgivings

Through the window my brother
and I watch Thanksgiving
drizzle in puddles
on Longwood Avenue.
The scrape of our Maker's
Marks across the laminate bar
sounds like the Bud I slid him
four Thanksgivings prior,
his shoulders slumped over
a stuffed crust slice since
the girl he loved dumped him
on her parents' porch
that morning. Today
the bartender dumps stuffing
with an ice cream scoop
into Styrofoam trays. Cranberries
bleed across potatoes burying
turkey. Shuttered stores in
the mall around us so silent
we hear the rocks clink in our
drinks as we wait for the gravy
to join the plastic bags
we'll haul to the hospital room
with our wives and my daughter,
fighting for breath in her bed.
He doesn't say he loves
me, nor I him. Instead
we tilt our shoulders
like we did as kids
over a plastic wheelbarrow
full of rainwater, stirring mud
and bark and grass blades
into soup. We push back
from the bar, square our
shoulders as one against

the gray drizzle over
this meal, this girl,
this hospital. Squinting
now at the bags, now at
the rain he describes it
like he did back then—
a delicious mess.

Two Better People

You wonder briefly if the kids down the hall in their dorm rooms can hear you. Five minutes after you lay your daughter in the crib and back away slowly, she jerks her head to the right, pulls her arm across her body, and screams. Eight days now she hasn't slept more than twenty minutes. Was this included when the doctors told you she's a 10 on the 1-10 scale of brain injuries?

You've tried the Ferber method and Babywise and Happiest Baby on the Block. What next? The neurologist was no help. She told you at your daughter's last appointment: "Sometimes babies cry." Your wife steps into the room and snatches your daughter from the crib. Carries her down the hall into the living room, bouncing and shushing. The rhythm is off. She's moving too fast. Three more bounces, and she thrusts her back in your arms as if she'd been hugging live wires.

She walks across the room to the light-up Sesame Street mirror. Picks it up, then turns and hurls it with all her might into the wall. Splinters of plastic rain to the floor. She takes a pink truck in both hands and plows it into the same spot. Follows it up with a small plastic piano. The wreckage smolders at her feet. Your daughter wails her rhythmic, duck-like *wahs*.

Scuffs of color mark the place where the toys struck the wall. The xylophone dog smashes into it as if it's a bullseye. An animal scream rises from your wife's throat. She takes fistfuls of her hair and pulls like she wants to tear her scalp down the middle. Like she wants to rip out her brain. She turns from the wall, away from the rainbow pile of shards. Falls to the floor. The gut-scream again. Her arms shaking with sobs, she begins to hit the floor with her open palm.

Her words come from a great distance: "I can't look at them. Throw them all away. They don't do any good. She'll never play with them." She sees you glance over your shoulder towards the dorm rooms—"I want them to hear. I want everyone to see this. I want them to hurt. I want them to be *sick*. What's the point? There is no point. I can't do this anymore. I can't do it." Her words become moans and then, "I can't do this. I'm going to leave. I can't bear it. You know why no one but my mom comes up here? Because it's no fun. It isn't any fun." She moans, rocks side to side, "The way I'd read to her, the way I'd play with her. She's never even going to know who we are. I'm never going to see her smile. I'm never going to see her laugh. She'll never look in my eyes." She wails softly for a few moments. "I'd have been such a good mother."

Your tongue grows heavy as your arms. There's no answer. No shield. Your daughter cries in your ear. You prop her in the corner of the couch and pour a tall glass of bourbon. Your wife pops three pills and slams the bedroom door. You click on the television, daughter in one arm and drink in the other, and settle there for the long night.

The next day at school as you tread heavy into the office, eyes black and sunken, your colleague asks how you're doing. You don't know how to answer. She shakes her head and tells you: "I can't think of two better people to face a challenge like this."

Velcro Ode

How wondrous when two
strips reach, their lips pursed,

ready to lock together:
partners stooping through

the loop to hook and hold
the other side. Opening

the velvet cockleburs
is a crowd's roar. Let us

take this tired flap, its last
frayed fibers clutching

over the tongue, and sing
how a five-inch square supports

an entire ton. How it clamps
a wound closed or attaches

watch to spacesuit for Armstrong's
steps on the moon. Or how it

helps a two-year-old so sick
she can't hold up her head

in her car seat, her chin pitching
down, closing her airway.

A simple thing, really. To breathe.
But hard to sustain sometimes

unless you know to kneel
and watch and listen

how breath halts and catches.
How the head tilts left before

falling forward. Riding along,
knowing this small thing you can

glue-gun strips to each arm
of a mini-airplane pillow

and glue partner patches
atop the car-seat straps, then

sandwich them to cushion chin
and cheek, which keeps her head up,

which in turn makes them lifelines
that may have clamped the caps

back onto bottles of Zoloft
and Vicodin her mom pondered

downing before learning she can
drive alone with her daughter

to support groups and doctor's offices
to orchards and aquariums

without risking her asphyxiation,
and so ripping open the cell door

of the apartment, taking
that first step out. A giant one.

Danvers State Mental Hospital

Inside the swim therapy building—
empty halls, bare walls, gray light.
Cranes at each shallow end
to lower their cargo
into over-chlorinated water.
My wife, dressing our daughter
in the locker room, watches
a nurse wrestle rumpled sweats
onto a young woman. *Like a gray straitjacket.*
Not even "Down by the Bay,"
hummed by our daughter's therapist,
softens the cracked tiles.

Outside, the road climbs toward the
abandoned asylum. Red brick towers.
Graves marked only by number.
In its overcrowded days, patients
slept in basements and tunnels.
Here at the edge of its campus,
this repurposed pool, the only one
shallow, warm, and close enough,
I step in the water carrying
our daughter. Her eyes are half-closed.
Two braids wrap her head like a crown.
Her pink tankini, lined with stars.
My wife glares at the walls,
the bricks, the road. In my ear
her soft growl, *We will never stop
dressing her in things that shine.*

Hypothermia Part 1

We're standing shoulder to shoulder amid the piles of seaweed on the West Beach shoreline. Almost the entire dorm is here. Some boys drape arms around one another, others jam fists in their short pockets or hoodies as we stare in silence across the gray waves to the green wall of trees on Misery Island. A mile off our shore. It happened last night, early evening. What drug or fever made Joe and Cory sail a small boat from a dock's safety in Manchester down the coast into four-foot seas?

It's my third year teaching. Cory was my student. He wrote with thick black ink, a gnarled script that reminded me of my own scrawling. He often arrived early to class, poked his maroon-dyed head horizontally into the door frame, then slouched to the corner desk—a wry grin on his face. He used the same move to enter our dorm kitchen where he had his own shelf of food. He was violently allergic to gluten.

When the Coast Guard found Joe huddled on the small beach on Misery Island, he told them how in the waves he screamed to Cory to leave the boat and swim for it. Cory was not a strong swimmer. He stayed with the boat and they said their last desperate goodbye.

Standing there, the May wind rustling our shorts, hypothermia seems it should be a thing for tundra and icebergs. A Jack London story or *Titanic*. Not something here and now off this shore.

When they found Cory in Salem harbor, he was still wearing his life jacket, still grasping the mast of the submerged boat. He had managed to avoid drowning, but his body had cooled beyond recovery or resuscitation. Sometimes clinging to a mast in the storm is not enough.

To the Vision Box

For Rose

which is a room
small enough to carry
made of plastic panes
and wooden stakes
that could tether tomatoes
nailed together by
our daughter's vision therapist
for small blind ones
learning to see

Lattice bells, pipe cleaners
and sticky rubber hands
reach from their low rafters
to caress the eyes
like car wash curtains

She kneels
beside our daughter
and pulls a blanket
over their heads
like a photographer
focusing light
that careens
off the plastic walls
and lands in a sky
hung with slices of
green and red moons

    then bends

back to the eye
in small portions
so it is not
quite
so dazzling.

Night Nurses

Though other night nurses sit at our dining room table to enter notes or rest until the next stat check, Kadeeja sits in our flower-embroidered rocker which she pulls close to our daughter's bedside. She watches over our son as well since he shares the room. She likes to pull back the curtain of the closest window to let the moon in. Says it is all the light she needs. When we ask her to switch to a Wednesday night, she agrees. My wife and I use the Tuesday hours for a daytime nurse to stay with our daughter while a close friend watches our son. We head to Hale Street for Tuesday night's half-price burgers. At home, we finish our daughter's respiratory therapies, administer the last of her meds, thank our nurse and babysitter and tuck in our children. Alone at last, we fall into bed for a few minutes finding hilarious glorious comfort in each other's breath and body and the darkness doesn't seem so thick. We stumble out of our bedroom, naked in the moonlit hallway, and make our way to the bathroom, pausing at the door of our daughter's room to peek at our sleeping kids. This is when we lock eyes with Kadeeja. Sitting in her usual rocker by our daughter's bedside, her long fingers covering her dropped jaw. Before we can wonder if it's her mistake or ours, before we can wonder how she made her way into the building or whether it really matters anyway, the three of us are frozen like that. She with her hand blanketing her mouth, my wife and I with our hands across our bodies. And maybe that's the nurses' role. Coming into our home to catch us raw and unguarded. Trying to help us through the long night.

After Two and a Half Years, Our Daughter Smiles

The therapeutic clouting
from our cupped hands
forms a rhythm.
A loosening inside her lungs.
The mountains of her pale cheeks
slowly, slowly straining.
The sweet corners of her mouth
begin to lift.

      Her face quakes open.
Deep in the fissure,
a kindling behind her eyes.
The light holds us.

2

Learning to See

For the Perkins School for the Blind
Infant-Toddler Program

Consider a diploma whose seal
is a pink star circled
by glittering hearts. Its tinfoil
background crinkles
beneath fingers and creates
pools of light in which
lavender crowns bloom
into sandpaper spikes.
Trace the thick-ridged border
where felt roses
blossom around stars
to witness this growth and grit.
Brush against a tufted feather
and frond of wisps that
like the glue binding
castles with buttons
is fixed by teachers
who noticed each eyebrow flex
and jaw clench.
Who laughed at each painted nail
as they took her hands
in theirs, then raised them
to our faces, turning us
from our gaze towards
the future. Telling us:
Stay here. Feel this.

Encomium is an Anagram of Meconium

Intestines today your dull writhing
is a song
processing
thirty feet through your halls
seeming simple until traffic jams
and we wait for release
let us praise how your seething
prods us closer
we hear our daughter scream
when you flare
you're a python
muscling our matter through
let us not *dis* but *em* bowel
origin from Latin mysterious
term for pudding or sausage
ribbed casing for the deepest parts
of feeling let us praise
the winding road for the shorter
does not break down
what must be broken
Uncharted territory her doctor calls
the twenty meds at war
in her three-year-old gut
MiraLAX softening and Senna
relaxing your constricted coils
move the letters this word for revel
becomes meconium
named for juice from the poppy
that cools what sears
if the dose is right
as it sometimes is
with the Morphine we give her
let us praise the ancient name
for tarry stool
remnant of womb's darkness

hard to wipe away
praise how that which gave us life
can be excreted
before it turns to poison

Hypothermia Part 2

I am standing in the dim evening light of the neonatal ICU. The technician glues dozens of EEG leads to my two-day-old daughter's scalp. She flinches. The famous neurologist is explaining the results of her MRI: *The brain is wondrous in its capacity to heal itself, but when the injury is global, when all its regions have been equally starved of oxygen …* He bows his head. I picture all the lights on all of the continents going dark. I picture a control room, screens and keyboards smoking. Below the gossamer veins on her eyelids, my daughter's lips purse. I take her soft fingers into mine.

One by one we see this injury palsy her body's systems. But her hypothermia keeps her in the NICU longest. At first, we take her temperature at every diaper change. As she grows older, we learn to watch her symptoms rather than constantly taking her temperature. Over and over, we place our palms to her cool chest. We touch our fingers to her cool cheek. Even so, we can still whip a thermometer from a drawer without looking, turn it on and stick it in the exact fold of armpit that yields the best temp. Of course, a rectal temp is often necessary for higher accuracy. We're experts in that, too.

Hypothermia is defined as less than 95 degrees. Our daughter runs between 93 and 94. Though symptoms vary depending on age and health, typically at this point someone fit and strong will experience severe shivering. Feel lethargic, apathetic, and become confused. Coordination will decrease while heart rate, respiratory rate, and blood pressure will increase. Muscles become rigid; eyesight and speech poor.

When her temperature dips to 93 and below, she sleeps. Until warming up, she will not be roused for appointments or playtime or anything. It also halts her bowels. Her temperature is too cold to melt a suppository.

We keep her bundled in pajamas, sweaters, robes, and blankets. We crank the heat in our apartment day and night. We avoid air-conditioning whenever possible, and when it isn't we bring twice the usual number of blankets and heating devices. We take big pink socks, fill them with rice, and make them into heating packs to accompany her electric one. We have three different space heaters. Our parents buy enormous space heaters for their houses, so she'll be warm enough when she comes to visit. We yearn for the return of hot weather. We decide to get involved with the

Make-A-Wish Foundation so that she might go somewhere hot enough to enjoy the outdoors without needing three to seven blankets.

A friend stops by to watch our young son, so we can take a walk with our daughter. Her blonde curls tumble out the back of her striped fleece hat. She pulls her head toward her left shoulder and yanks her right fist free of her heavy pink wrappings. She stretches her big toes so the fluff of her insulated socks pops out beneath the blankets. She pulls her head left again and a pink tassel on her fleece hat catches against the headrest of her Kid Kart, pushing it down over her eyes. My wife reaches out and adjusts it. Our daughter rolls her eyes to the right and focuses them in the direction of gull's cries and boat engines and surf softly singing.

We weave our way around the parking lot potholes and onto the cement walkway overlooking the beach. We tuck in her blankets against the breeze and look across the strip of sand, across the ocean channel to Misery Island. We know limbs lose warmth as the body prepares to die. We know the cold is coming for her.

My wife brushes the backs of her fingers against our daughter's cheek. Then she turns and stretches her palm up to place it on my forehead. *You're so warm,* she says. When our other children arrive, we will touch them the same. Almost greedily. With wonder. When they climb onto our laps and lean their heads to our chests, our hands and skin will feel scorched. Again and again we will reach, feeling the miraculous heat of their bodies.

This is who we are now, following our hands to heat like dowsing rods to water. We will return home, and our son will teeter up to us. We will reach out our hands and feel the warmth in his cheek and forehead. The cool of her cheek in one cupped hand, the warmth of his like fever in the other. Like we're sitting too close to the fire.

Assist

Our two-year-old's team
of ICU doctors is explaining
they're sending us home with
a cough assist machine. I hear
the word *assist* and can't help
but see Magic as he whips
a one-handed pass full court
over the hands of a defender
to hit Worthy in stride
for the game-winning dunk.
I remember mimicking
the way Jalen flicked his wrists
to float the ball over the rim
for C-Webb's waiting hands.
But here before us is this weapon
of breath we must wield
to help our daughter expel
the junk from her lungs.

The doctors prescribe five sets
of five. I joke it's a game
of fives. Full court. Before we turn
to the machine with its dials
and its inhale and exhale thumps
we swap her oxygen mask for the
nebulizer mask with fish eyes
and orange scales. We squeeze in
drops of meds that form a cloud
she breathes to loosen the rubble
in her lungs. Then my wife makes
one hand into a cup and whacks
rhythmically on her chest, back,
and ribs. They call it Chest PT.
For fifteen minutes
our daughter becomes our drum

and the bump and thrum of our hands
on her flesh becomes a song.
Her eyes open wide with hushed
focus; she smiles in delight,
and for a few holy moments
there is nothing else in the world.

Halloween Parade, Children's Hospital Boston

Waving in our doorway, a tiny Tom Brady
wheeled by a nurse with Ortiz's 34 and eye black.
And of course there's royalty—Tiana, Fiona,
Rapunzel—pouring down the hall.
Even the king from Burger King
limps near the nurses' candy station.

The casters on their IV poles squeak
to techno beats bouncing off the tiles
in this wing for injured brains and struggling lungs.
My daughter rustles under her sheets,
nudges her globe of light
atop a scepter matching theirs.

Peering in our door a small skeleton,
bones outside his skin glowing neon.
Behind him a taller figure, cloaked and shadowed.
Make no mistake: our kids are hiding
from Death, who long has prowled these halls.
They're tucking behind hero masks,
stretching the nylon in disguise.

My daughter's mask shovels oxygen to her lungs,
green strap squeezing her cheek,
blue tube like an elephant's trunk.
She nudges the glowing wand again,
pushing back the shadow with a little bit of glitter.

Instructions for Deep Suction

After Natasha Trethewey

Just breathe when you press the cough assist mask
over your daughter's nose and open mouth,
its thick tubing like a tentacle's grip.

On her faint exhale, click the switch that blasts
the air into her lungs. Withdraw the mask
and grip between thumb and forefinger the long thin

tube of pliable plastic that provokes her cough.
If you don't, it's back to pneumonia, back
to the hospital, and then, soon, death.

Learn to ignore the way her hands fly from her knees
to shoulder high as if to fend you off
while you thread the tube, dipped in Surgilube,

up her nose and down her throat. When she chokes
at the invasion of oxygen, tell yourself
her numbers are back in a range you'd almost

call normal. Keep going as her face turns
scarlet and her eyes bulge. Remember your
work and pride in learning this procedure,

your wife's praise for your steady hands.
As the secretions strangle up and out, call her
gasps for breath success: *You did it, sweet one.*

Place your hand to her forehead while you pull
the tube back out and tell her to rest. Lay
your hand on her chest, click the suction off,

and avoid dwelling on the words of her
kindest doctor: *There's almost no limit
to how complex the full-court press can get.*

Remind yourself there is no future ten
years distant where she'll talk through this
suffering with a trusted therapist.

When stimulating a cough takes more tries,
remind yourself that palliative care allows these
invasions along with her comfort. Fight the urge

for the hundredth time to ask *how long can
we keep doing this*? As you watch your daughter drift
to sleep, let go again the thought you can protect

her. Don't imagine yourself as a shield
between her and the tubing's tentacles.
Don't imagine a door she escapes through,

tearing the mask from her face, ripping the cords
from the machines and walking away free.

When the Conference Room Where We are to Plan Our Daughter's Death Looks Like the Room Where We Learned of Her Brain Injury

Our social worker stands so quick
her chair rocks back on two legs
before we think to ask
she moves the meeting
to the garden

For Marsha Joselow

The Extraction Team

For Sarah & Andrew Frey

The job is simple: stand in front
of an avalanche and break it
into steady streams. As the discharge
process stretches from morning
to late afternoon, we make the call
from our daughter's hospital bed.
They respond in a montage.
A phone hoisted to an ear.
Books fly from hands.
Gear thrown in a duffle:
knitting needles and salad tongs
a tattered fantasy novel
marinated chicken breasts.
This time the extraction will take place
on a bridge heavy with tanks
and machines they'll help haul
from the van to our apartment
where instead of working
like they did in the hospital
there is the error beep
from the feeding pump,
the suction machine's bloated groan.
The pulse oximeter clangs
at our daughter's raised finger.
They holster a Malbec bottle
in a brown bag. A six-pack clinks
in one hand, the other ready
to pour oil in the pan,
fiddle with the dials, or
hold our rasping little girl,
so we can thumb through
the hospital instructions

and call the triage doctors.
We scan the manual to attach
the nozzle and connect tubes
to the oxygen for our child
who even if she recovers
will not recover. As they lever bar blades
to their bottle crowns, they quip
how they'll wedge the necks
to our molars and pry loose
the abscessed things wanting to die.

Chucks

For Jen Gamble

1.

When shit leaves our daughter's body
we describe it as natural
disaster: eruption, tsunami, flood
during hospital stays
for aspiration pneumonia.
The strong antibiotic requires
blankets and towels for makeshift dams,
no saving the white sheets.

You go girl! her nurse cheers beside us,
pulling the sheets from their corners.
She spread the river wide this time I offer
as she grabs the small pink tub
to soak the strawberry cargos
and she laughs, unfurls a new square pad
and calls it *a chuck. So you can chuck it
in the wash or the trash.*
A canvas, my wife and I agree,
for the next masterpiece.

She arrives to check vitals
with a new stack of sheets, clean chucks,
another pink tub. At shift change
we ask when she's working next.
Two days later she walks in nodding
at the new tubs soaking
our daughter's soiled clothes:
*The tubs multiplied! You're talented,
Pooh Bear*, tickling our daughter's arm.
She rolls the computer cart

into our room to chat while typing,
and when our daughter next needs
the hospital, we hope to see her,
so the stay might feel bearable.

2.

It's true that laughing about shit
is a gut-deep mercy
if your nurse's joke, *You saved it
all for me? I'm honored!*
is followed hours later
by unwiped tears
as she points to our daughter's
belly and chest straining
for rapid shallow breaths,
clanging monitors confirming
oxygen dropping and respiration too fast,
her tears telling us more
than the doctor's phrases
about the move to the ICU: *tired,
working to breathe, needs more support.*
When we sat in the hospital garden a year later
and planned our daughter's death,
we asked for her as our nurse
and a special room at Children's.
She made the bed we requested,
but our daughter never got there.
We imagine her nurse after
learning the news
stacking the empty pink tubs,
putting away the chucks,
clean and unsoiled.

The Blanket on the Bench

The week before our daughter dies, a woman from *Now I Lay Me Down to Sleep* comes to our apartment to click candids of the light on her eyelashes and her fingers loosely clutching her teddy bear and the manicured big toe she tips into the air while crinkling the others. The photographer kneels down and captures the final poses of our family dressed up together. Outside our dorm is a patio that looks out over the ocean and there against a cloudless sky we sit on a wooden bench for a barrage of shots. She snaps a photo of our daughter's pink blanket, left behind on the empty splintered slats, hanging its head over the bench, splashing its pink hues against the brown of the wood, the green of the lawn, the ocean gleaming in the sunlight.

My Sisters Paint My Dying Three-Year-Old's Nails

a chair near the shore
her fingers in the palm of
my sister-in-law

as she dusts pink coasts
along nails drying
the color of sunset

my sister's light strokes
brush across her toenails
making green fields

for flowers she paints
like commas pausing mid-breath
the sentence, carving

our rebuke to walls
of state hospitals, green
against the gray

creeping in her skin
a song dabbed against the drab
even if we think

of new heavens and a new
earth, of arms clasped round necks
her painted nails linger

in the earth
flowers in the field

The Morning After My Daughter's Death, Cleaning Out Her Med Cabinet

After Ted Kooser

I can't explain my rush
(family slumped in couches,
sister-in-law heaped on the floor,
mom cracking eggs into a bowl)
in opening the kitchen hutch
we assembled then repurposed last year.
It's the old world now:
feeding pump bags, suction catheters,
neb masks painted with smiling fish faces,
and the deep top shelf
from which I grab ten bottles,
line them up on the counter,
soldiers awaiting sentence.
I twist off the Ativan cap and pause
as if to draw two mL's
and press them through her G-tube
to quell her brain
from sparking into seizures.

Glugging into the toilet:
red-tinged Neurontin,
Morphine like maple syrup,
white globs of Topamax mixed
by a pharmacist two towns over
who spent days fine-tuning the recipe.

Maybe I'm afraid I'll try each one
like I sampled her food and treatments,
trying to taste what she couldn't tell us.
Maybe I'm afraid I'll stash them.
Maybe because, waking

from Benadryl-soaked sleep
I forgot for a second she died
and the knowledge swirled back,
trying to flush away
the dream that she's alive.

Grief

An orca nudges forward
her daughter, small
sinking body.

Skin to skin she carries her
across her shoulders
mile after mile carving
days into weeks.

If the body begins to fall,
she catches it,
rising through the water
as if pushing a ball
to the surface.

Then one day
the daughter's body
slides from her back
again. The mother
lets her drift

and turns away
into an endless sea

Lacing 'Em Up

You should lace 'em up &
come back out with us
the Upper School director
says as if he knows
how you sneak from
the dorm apartment
weeks after
your daughter's funeral
dodging eyes that turn
and park on you.
Maybe it's time to slip
into backdoors and jab-
steps amid the soles'
sweet squeak
on hard maple boards.
You shield your eyes from
squares of sunlight
between the arc and key,
pivot to find
both ball and man—
the familiar shuffle
and slide. The only talk,
Screen on your left, switch,
then the steal and outlet
pebbled leather
finding your fingers
before an orange halo.
Leap and leave this earth
and the wood
will catch you as you return.

Pink Feather Boa

She is pinching my son's
small thumb and index finger

around the petals of a
buttercup, chanting

She loves me; she loves me not
flecking them windward

over the row of graves
and onto the windshield.

We noticed her
when we parked facing

this grassy corridor,
the sun behind her blazing

through a sheen of haze
to make her a tall silhouette

kneeling to knot a balloon
to the potted plant beside

our daughter's headstone—
the only care left to give

her patient. After we
revised the DNR form

and our daughter began hospice
our longest tenured night nurse

never showed again. So Diane
shouldered the extra hours,

and later stepped to the podium
wearing a pink feather boa

at our daughter's funeral
to speak of the lightness

she felt when holding her.
She loves me; she loves me not,

crouching beside the headstone,
pulling a stray from our son's cheek.

With the same motion she
reached for an oral syringe

he plucked off the drying rack while
she was laying out the evening meds.

He dangled it between his lips
as if it were a smoke and

as he flings the next petal
she chuckles the way she did

when she closed the cabinet doors
my wife left ajar, slight shake

of her head, placing the Neurontin
next to the Morphine on the counter.

And yes she did walk us
through the door of our daughter's

last breath, held a stethoscope
to her chest and confirmed

her heart beat no longer.
And at 2 am, her tall shadow

thrown by sconces on the
walls outside our apartment

she walked away alone.
Our son gasps. He's out of petals

and her laugh climbs into
a whooping peal. Tears

gather in her eyes as if
she's drawing the Morphine again

into a clean oral syringe
and like all good nurses

pressing it gently through the tube.

3

West Beach

Sometimes life is the long-winged gull
that dips its beak into your tote,
retreating to a rock in the waves
with your Ziploc of sandwiches
it cannot penetrate, neither of you
tasting the raspberry jam
spread just to the edge.

Sometimes at low tide the finger of beach
spreads into a playground.
Pillars from a rotted pier lean
toward the sea. Snaking past them, tracks
like those our daughter's wheelchair carved
when we caravanned out
amid the towels and umbrellas.

After her death, the empty beach invites our two-year-old
to gallop against the soft sand.
Before we can catch him, he grasps the gray wing
of a gull's carcass.
Saying hello.

Pass It On

My daughter is sixteen now the guy with bushy white hair from Pass It On tells us, squatting to inspect our daughter's Kid Kart. *She has cerebral palsy, and she's on her fourth chair like this. When they outgrow them too quickly or insurance won't cover, this can save families more than ten grand.*

I find myself picking up the IV pole attachment and the Ziploc of spare parts and holding the apartment door open as my wife wheels our daughter's Kid Kart into the hall outside our apartment. *We'll find it a good home,* he says.

As I swing in behind her, there's no way to see that the Kid Kart is empty. We could be taking her for a walk or a swing. To school or a friend's house. The wheels have worn a slight track in the hallway carpet.

The last time we loaded her Kart into a strange van, we were taking her to Disney World. Her chauffeur was wearing a tux. This time it rolls into place beside old standers and wheelchairs. He bungees it with the others.

We want to line it with her blankets and equipment, string a spiral mobile with bulbs gleaming from its visor, park it in a row beside the chairs of her classmates, not leave it cramped in the dim cargo light and grime of this old van, waiting to be hauled away.

He closes the door, turns and sees our faces.

He says, *Sometimes I hate this job.*

New Neighborhood

For Mark and Sybil Coleman

1)

The first land we purchase
is our daughter's grave.
The funeral director gave the tour:
spacious, two plots, plenty of light.

2)

Our son jets water into a plastic half-gallon
braced two-handed against his thigh
to slosh over the mums. The jug's
almost as big as he is. He stops
four plots down for Legos
parked beside baseballs
on the black granite ledge.

3)

Our daughter's neighbor is a rope
coiled on a cross. It's a guy
I taught with. Died the year
she was born. With salt in his grumble
showed kids to sand the wood and seal
the hull with skill so few still know.
I picture his hand on her shoulder,
backs to us, peering across the sea.

4)

At their sister's grave my sons ask,
Is this stone where she is?
Is heaven underneath the ground?
How do you breathe down there?
Can we dig down to see her?
Can I die so I can go see her?

5)

The unicorn balloon from her third birthday
unfurls atop her plot. Our hands scoop
beads and Silly Bands from her jewelry box.
My wife's mom opens a bag of Tootsie Pops
and our younger son tucks one in each
cheek pocket. Our older son strays
to the tree at our row's end, drags
a stick along the fence bars
like a barker calling patrons.

6)

I'm sprawling on my back behind
the double-wide tombstone at
the cemetery's farthest edge.

Our kids' screams echo over
footsteps thudding on turf
in the noontime heat.

Then a low shadow and a cluck.
Chickens darting between graves
escaped the neighbor's yard again.

A figure blocks out the sun.
Found you! my son calls down.
Now it's my turn to count.

7)

We look up from our blanket
by her headstone to see our kids
and their cousins climbing two tombs
looming across the grass corridor.
They wait in line for a turn to tumble
down the hill like puppies
in the old book we'd read her.

8)

Four hydrangeas mark the garden's corners
near the tall gate where our kids dance
on small stone plinths, shaking their hips.

9)

From the graveyard corner
crossed Civil War rifles
guard the monument's stair.

A cannon spans its summit,
barrel black in the sunlight.
Then a scrape of nails.

Into the air above it
a claw, forearm, elbow,
and our son's blonde spikes.

He swings his Nikes
astride the muzzle, clutches an
invisible saddle, snaps the reins.

10)

The tomb doors' bolts blued with age. Flowers sprout
through cracks in their red brick crowns. Above them
seven cousins hunch like cartoon animals on a greeting card.
Their shadows lengthen across the grass below,
touching the fallen bricks the mortar could not hold.

11)

Fallen hydrangea blossoms ring the headstone grass.
They ring the pink ledge, crest the pink granite.

My niece brings two more in each hand.
One good gust will scatter them but until then

this cloud of blossoms wraps the stone
like lilac dresses she and my daughter once wore.

Typing this my finger slips
from *v* to *c,* turns *grave* to *grace.*

Mustard Seeds

At the Children's Hospital memorial service a year after our daughter's death, a pediatrician speaks into the mic: *Three years ago, Mark and I lost our baby boy and this parable has comforted us.* The man beside her puts his hand on her back. I need a second to recognize his good hair, his parade-ground posture. It's our favorite respiratory therapist, wearing a shirt and tie instead of scrubs.

She reads, *Kisa Gotami wrapped the little body in its baby sheet and carried it to her neighbor's door.* I'm in the two-a.m. light of my daughter's hospital room again. *"Please, my friend," Kisa Gotami begged, "give me some medicine that will cure my child."* Mark is at my elbow, unspooling the blue tube and taking a suction catheter from its wrapping. *But when her neighbor lifted the sheet and saw the baby's face, she knew he had died. No medicine could cure him.* I lean over, patting my daughter's side with a cupped hand. Her sweet dry breath. Its damp echo in her chest.

Finally, a man on the street told her to visit Buddha. She hurried there and asked for medicine. Buddha looked at her tenderly, "My good woman, you must help me find the medicine. Go and bring me a handful of mustard seed, but remember this: The mustard seed must be taken from a house where no one has ever died or it will be of no use."

Mark clicks on the cough assist; it drones like a vacuum. He looks at me, speaks slow like he moves, "Go ahead and rest. Try to get some sleep. I'll take it from here." He reaches across my daughter's bed, slips off the nasal cannula, presses the mask to her face. Every pulse of breath Mark gave her, he gave knowing a child's quiet once breath is gone.

She gently laid her child's body on its little bed and went to find the handful of mustard seed. At every door it was the same. There was no house in all the village where someone had not died.

I lift my eyes to the packed auditorium. Some wear t-shirts and sweats. Others wear dresses, suits, ties. Some in hijabs, others in shawls and tassels. A few glittering cloaks and studded collars.

In the Lobby

My son approaches the toy box the way he approaches life: head first and full speed. His head and shoulders disappear into the wooden chest and plastic clatters against wood. Out fly my daughter's old toys: the snail that lights up and sings; the quilted lizard with crinkly paws; the pink four-legged massager. He emerges, holding high the elephant whose belly is a mirror that spins a singing mouse, drops it in my lap.

Suddenly I'm at a table in the lobby of Children's Hospital, peering over the top of my computer screen at an elephant perched on a bird's nest. I'm nine floors below the wing that was our second home during her life. Beside the elephant is a painting of orange swans trumpeting past a man on a one-tree island in the setting sun. I realize that I'm sitting in the midst of a Dr. Seuss gallery. There is a painting of a fish surrounded by other fish, a bust of a kangaroo-bird, a sculpture of a "semi-normal green-lidded fawn."

I walk over and pause before a piece titled, "Every Girl Should Have a Unicorn." The aromas of broccoli-cheddar soup and Asiago bagels drift over from Au Bon Pain. In the din of the lobby, I can hear the cries and laughter of children amidst the conversations of parents in a dozen languages. Kids press their noses to the glass around the kinetic ball sculpture, leaving prints that blur into other prints. The *clang* and *bong* and whirling gears of the perpetual "Bippity-Boppity Balls" echo like a greeting from an old friend. And now I can feel again the rubber grips of my daughter's wheelchair beneath my palms.

My son pulls an oxygen mask out of his toy box. He always wanted to play with her equipment, most of which we didn't allow because of the danger to both of them. But the blue tubing that carried the moisturized oxygen to her lungs doubled as a trumpet, and the extra oxygen masks could be part necklace or part headgear.

This time he hands it to me, grasping the nylon band with two fingers as if he's dangling a mouse by the tail. I take it from him gently, extending both of my hands. I do what comes naturally: slide my palm along the inside of the band until it is stretched out far enough to slide it down over my daughter's head and her lion's mane and fit it onto her face. And I can feel her soft curls.

Soul Stone

Perhaps a gem with power over souls is
the heart of a god that died, but more
likely it was in the god's bowels where time
and pressure smoothed the jagged surface

before excreting it. For our daughter,
taking the edge off meant extra doses
of morphine. My wife and I nestle
against the couch's soft leather and watch

two heroes pause at a precipice seeking
a rock that requires only life to pay for life.
We know what will happen: Black Widow
and Hawkeye will kick and claw to be the one

running toward the cliff and plunging
over the edge. A thousand times we've seen it.
We do not believe in bitter trades; we did not
offer what we love most to Molech's jaws. And yet

our daughter slides into the pink-dotted hoodie
of a sister she's known only in photos.
And yet I sing night upon night
to the ones alive the lullabies I sang

to the one who died. Smoothing the edge.
Now my wife and I both are bolted to the cliff
with Hawkeye, clutching Black Widow's hand
as she says *Let me go*. Watching her fall.

Standing In It

I stop stacking the kids' bikes at the song from the garage boombox:
Slip sliding away. Slip sliding away. You know the nearer your destination
the more you're slip sliding away. I sang this clad in swim trunks,
carrying my firstborn to the tub. It's been years since she died,
but there's her rubber duck thermometer confirming
the water's 101 degrees. Suction machine beside the tub if she struggles.
I'm cradling her with my left arm, bracing my descent with my right.
We drop the last few inches into water that rolls away and rebounds over our laps.

She tenses against the water's touch and then reclines, head against my hands,
peeking under long lashes, mouth corners turned up. The pressure lifts
from her limbs, weightless in the rocking water, and Marley pours from me:
Oh Please, don't you rock my boat. Cause I don't want my boat to be rock-ed.
Her head on my forearm, I take the pre-soaped washcloth and scrub
around the port to her stomach. Her eyes bright and focused, her cheek
not too cold. An eyebrow arched. Her hair floating around her face.

I massage in shampoo and shift to a hymn's tune—*Waaash-ing.*
Waaaash-ing. We are washing Charlotte's hair. She stiffens her arms
and blinks, relaxes again as I rinse the soap and glide my fingers
through her hair. She hovers there, still and quiet in the soap-clouded water.
A few wisps drift like jellyfish. They might be bits of mucus or soap
or debris from a tub not quite clean enough. And then in the particles
I see brown flecks. She jets two ropes into the murk and my cry, *Oh shit!*
rings like a command and her warm, calm body gives way
to the stool softener and doses of Senna to relax her intestines and
the nineteen other meds in her system, and she unleashes the rest.

Slip sliding away. Here in the garage, what lingers isn't shit and water
running from my hands and bathing suit down my legs
into the pool of shit and water. It isn't her nurse, Sharon,
hauling the door open and crouching with a towel beside the tub as I heave
my huge three-year-old up out of the mess or the slick exchange
where she slips from my grasp, and Sharon half-falls half-catches her
an inch from the floor. What lingers is song. *Waaash-ing.*
Waaaash-ing. We are washing Charlotte's hair. Floating. Weightless.

Breaking My Favorite Mug

After Naomi Shihab Nye

Even after
the kitchen floor
stops its falling
its blue patterns gallop
in ranks across
the linoleum

I held it
while I held her
Now gone

so much is breaking

It was handed to us
by old friends
who live up the street
from the graveyard
holding our
daughter's body

among the three largest pieces
the handle crooks
towards me
asking

For John and Laurie Truschel

West Beach Again

A pigeon rope-a-dopes within my youngest daughter's reach,
but her gaze lifts toward the jetty stones and tidal pools

and gulls' wings, two commas against the horizon.
Beneath them, my son drags a tuna carcass from

two slick rocks through the wet sand. It's taller
than she is. Their footprints are deep beside it.

He caresses the jaw, still fleshed enough to attract
two vultures. She traces her fingers along the tail.

Why are my children drawn to death in places clumsy with life?
The circle they dig around the body mirrors

the vultures' slow descent. The vultures wait
until my kids climb back on the kelp-coated rocks.

Fake Zombies

Those clouds look like God's face.

*If there was a shooting star, I'd wish
we could be infinity best friends.*

It feels like my tooth is beeping. My tooth has brain freeze!

My brother's voice sounds like the morning.

*Rees took his superman costume and threw it in the trash,
so someone else could use it. Are you writing that down?*

I'm going to drive up to the sky and flip off.

*I wish we were in heaven. There would be no virus, no flies,
it's always summer, and we can have super powers.*

Do you like your life right now?

Why do you always write down the things I say, Dad?

I am very déjà vu.

When you did that, Dad, your face looked just like a normal boy.

If you turn into a grown-up, Dad, you can have that.

Did you know this is my first time being alive?

Did you know if you didn't have any ears, you wouldn't get the chance to hear?

Did you know that fake zombies are real?

*What does God look like?
I think God looks like everyone.*

*You're still a kid, Dad, because you'll
always be a kid since you have a dad.*

Can you make me in your journal?

To the Flour Handprints on My Wife's Pants

whose traces appear
signs that
some spectral being
alighted here
to rest her hands
atop the curved shelf
below her hips
a ghost self
who lost only the syrup
and maybe her car keys
the rest here and whole
no bitter herbs
with the zucchini
shredded to nourish
her children
in a small kitchen
where our butts brush
flecks of flour
rise from black leggings
lingering there
a message chalked on slate
from a dimension
where all our children are alive
together in the portrait
above the dining room table
where when we catch
each other's eyes
mid-sentence mid-laugh
through the wisps
of our daughter's hair
it isn't only fantasy
all four sets of hands present
in the upside-down artwork
five braids of rope dangling

from each paint-dipped palm
grooved and blotched
clouds we'd like to climb

A Difficult Stick

It's flu season, so lunch talk turns
to shots. Stories flit from injection
to blood draw or donation:
who bruises, who faints, who hides
when the needle's steel angles toward you,
primed so a drop drips like slaver
from a rabid tooth. *It's like this,*
our school nurse says, *you've gotta chatter
like a hair dresser—then strike quick.*

What I know I do not say:
night in the neonatal ICU.
My daughter's faint arm veins outlined
in red light. The beam hovers
like a UFO searching surfaces
to land its needle. My fingers
comb her clotted hair, the remnants
of her birth not yet washed away.

She's a difficult stick, her nurse
tells another, as if my daughter's
a limb protruding from a tree,
a bough breaking. It means
they'll keep scanning the river
of her skin with their flashlights
and cast their needles in,
veins retreating like timid fish.
If they catch one, it'll be too small
to fill the tubes or carry
the saline and be released.
They'll move from her arms to pierce
her wrists and feet while her wounded cells
limp through her arteries,
gray and silent in the spotlights
of the NICU at night.

At the table, talk touches on those
who each day inject insulin.
A friend pulls up a chair and tells
of a random blood clot in his lung:
Got my blood drawn each week.
What I know I do not say.
I could never sighs one dad,
fork clicking on the plastic plate,
scooping up teriyaki chicken.
He passed his fear of shots to his son
who passed out before the Tetanus
booster. My left neighbor is quiet
and perhaps recalls the summer
in college, steadying her hands
to draw blood at the local hospital.
How to cross this distance?

I see little feet and hands taped
to a foam and vinyl board securing
an IV catheter. Her fingers
spill over the splint's edges
like ivy outgrowing its pot
as they push the good blood in.

And now we're in the yellowing
light of the Coordinated Care wing,
brushing tears with the tips of our thumbs
from her two-year-old eyes.
She stiffens her arm at the cold swab,
tries to pull it from the nurse's grip.
We don't know this nurse though we know
to say, *She's a difficult stick,*
our index fingers raised. She seems
surprised at our interruption;
she knows she must break through,

so the meds and nutrients can enter.
We know forty thousand miles
of vessels flow through our daughter
with no easy port of entry.
And if you don't stop them,
some nurses will keep trying
until they start digging.

At the table, what I know
I do not say: once there were five
different spinal taps. *If at first you don't
succeed*—this was the ER doctor
because procedure mandates it
to rule out Meningitis
when a temperature's too low.
The needle grows as I watch
from behind my plate, teriyaki
tinged with antiseptic. It again
approaches her pale back, the curve
of her small spine pressing through her skin
as they hunch her forward
on the bed, feeling the muscles
of my own back clenching
tighter than my fist around my fork,
heat stabbing my tear ducts.

To my right, she dabs napkin
to lips, pushes back her chair.
Beside her, my friend frets
his forearm scars beneath his sleeve.
He digs a shovelful of florets
from his salad, knifes a small tomato.
Another with laugh and shrug
talks of her husband's dental chair—
how he only brings the needle near

when patients lean back,
so they don't see it approaching.

I don't say how two boys sit
arm-to-arm in a brick wall's shade.
The taller one's eight and carrying
a brain tumor. He's an old teacher
of those fearing blood draws and leans
towards my six-year-old, showing him
how to smooth the white paste
up a trembling forearm and numb the spot
before the needle punctures. He nods
at the lab upstairs: *It stinks but it'll be ok.*
Just don't look at the needle.

But here at the table, that's what
I'm trying to say. How we can look
from its plunger down the barrel
to the hub where the needle emerges
and not turn away. How we can look
along its edge and keep our gaze there
until its tapered point opens
and we see the little reed
through which the blood is removed
or what we need is delivered.

Across the table the seats are now vacant.
Cold gusts breathe through dining hall windows.
Soon staff will upend the chairs, place them
on the table and begin to sweep.
Fork poised between plate and mouth,
on my tongue there's one last scene.
If you'll pull up a chair.

Ridges of carpet carve into my knees.
Afternoon sun staggers
through our living room window.
Beside me kneels a nurse named Nicole.
We're at my daughter's feet
listening to the beep that tells us
her feeding is finished, hoping
hydration and heating pads will
waken the blood she's here to draw.

A difficult stick? she asks and we nod.
She traces her brown fingers
up my daughter's pale forearms,
hums "Amazing Grace." She laughs,
delighted when our daughter pulls away
to rest her chin on the opposite hand.
Feeling for the veins again, she
stretches her arms out, slow,
with our daughter's, like dancers,
and tucks them back into wings.
Only then does she wrap the tourniquet.
Delicate. Humming again she holds
the red beam close, so it shines through
the skin. Placing a thumb beside
the site she's chosen, she looks up
from the arm to our daughter's face
as she uncaps the needle,
and back to the arm
then back to the face
as she slides the needle home.

Our daughter juts her bottom lip
as the band unclips from her
bicep, and she grinds her voice
into one short wail. Trails it

with a whimper and a single tear
and it's then we see the tears
behind Nicole's glasses.
She fills the tube and caps it,
and this gift she gave us
I give to you.

I'm Writing a Tornado

Dad, look! We found a mystery!
Can you write me in your journal, too?
I am happening.
Yesterday I got blood.
My fear hurts.
Did you know if you don't have a mouth you can breathe through your nose cause God
will always let you have a mouth? Unless you're mean.
Do you know God doesn't want everything to be chopped down?
The directions always know where to go.
I think the wind is me.
Dad, I can't wake my eyes up.
This is my friend, purple.
Sometimes I have a beard on my face.
I found this. It's called pink.
My name should be Songmaker.
My mouth does not like these peas.
Mom uses this pen to tattoo her lips.
I want you to throw me up into the sky.
Those two people were not holding hands—that's dangerous.
After today, guess what? It's tomorrow!
I am sleeping in this cozy mess.
I don't know the words in this book, but they're pretty good.
Everyone in this family is a maker:
they are all good at making.

Sneezing

Why do we sneeze? My son
asked the other day,
watching me wince
at his nasal blast.
His question is about
more than reflex so I ask,
Remember the girl at equine therapy?
About four years old?
He replies slowly, *With*
your students? I nod.
Rain pinged the tin roof
above the riding ring
where one held the reins
and one walked on each side,
hands raised like they just returned
Lady Gaga to the stage.
She was sneezing, right? he asks.
He's right—not nimble enough
to cover her mouth when grasping
the saddle, she sprayed down.
Something in her tenuous perch,
resplendent pink helmet and glasses,
calming her arm spasm.
Something in my students' smiles,
hands still uplifting,
flinching only slightly in the shower,
so much like my dead daughter's therapists
when they held her,
pulled me from my seat
and out the door into the rain.
Beyond the eaves, water sliding
down the roof, I wept.
Then something pressed against
my lower back. Small arms
circled my waist. And this is the part

I'm trying to tell him: The reflex
that made him follow me out the door,
take his small warm arms,
and hug me there in the rain
makes me think the old belief
that a sneeze is the soul leaving
the body isn't entirely wrong.
*Maybe the body is expelling what it needs
to expel*, I tell him. *Maybe sometimes
the soul needs to become rain
or the warm arm in the rain.*
Kind of weird, he says.

Upon Hearing the Animals One Mile into a Long Day's Drive Back to My PA Hometown

After John Murillo

Plans for seeing folks and routes to get there get lost
in the vocals: *There is a house* and a house shimmers

on my mind's ridge. Morning sun smolders behind the fog
stretching from Talcott Mountain. The house is empty

but its garage holds a boombox and a kerosene can
my wife's dad would empty into campfires. Two crows

leap from a squirrel's body on the double-yellow line
and I fret my leap from house to garage to fire. This

is about a song and the song has long since ended
but the notes climb with me onto the walled-rock roads

of the highway's next mountains. *I'm goin' back,* Burdon sings.
What collapses life to a house like that? We're around a fire

when I first hear my wife's father play it, somewhere
between *Mustang Sally* and *Ring of Fire*, and somewhere

beneath his mustache, beneath silver chest hair
spilling from a half-buttoned black shirt, he slides fret

to fret mixing in songs he wrote for each daughter
and grandchild. My eldest's shoulders and large hands

unclenched upon hearing, *My mother she was a tailor,*
she sewed my new blue jeans, the strings' twang echoing

across the flames to this long road
of memory. In Joan Baez's cover she urges

shun that house, her voice reaching back
to the version sung by miners and their

daughters, before it told of *many a poor boy,*
back when its name was *Rising Sun Blues,*

back in lonely towns at dawn in the fog
when a girl was lost, a ruinous house

snatching her future away. Quiet in the car but still
the strings echo from my father-in-law's guitar.

He has stopped singing.
I can't do this, he says—words we all have said

at one time or other—which is similar to words
my dad spoke two weeks before my eldest died

when he prepared to cover her small cool brow
with baptismal waters. And then he did it.

But here on the night of her death my father-in-law
sits on her bed and strums this crowd favorite

as she lies on my lap, her *one foot on the platform,*
her *other foot on the train,* all of us there

to see her off, her hair trailing against the flowers
on the rocker, our hands in its softness,

the beat driving slowly as we massage her chest,
caress her calves, her large hands clenching

and my wife's father thrumming the chords
to this house of grief, this song of a girl undone

driving us back to ballads in sixteenth-century
ale houses, back to Appalachian mines, deep into

roots of folk and lore and out into the fields,
into the blues, traveling all that distance

to enter the room through his fingers, past midnight
our cries mingling with his. Half howl, half prayer.

    For Nick

My Three-Year-Old Wears the Shirt Her Older Sister Wore the Day She Died at Three Years Old

peace in plastic diamonds
purple roses sprouting flames
pink leopard print
joining wings the color of sky

Notes

Many pantoums, my "She Exits the Womb as Though on a Gurney" included, have been inspired and influenced by Natalie Diaz's "My Brother at 3 A.M."

"Instructions for Deep Suction" is after Natasha Trethewey's "Imperatives for Carrying On in the Aftermath."

"The Morning After My Daughter's Death, Cleaning Out Her Med Cabinet" is after Ted Kooser's poem, "After the Funeral."

"Breaking My Favorite Mug" is after Naomi Shihab Nye's "Breaking My Favorite Bowl."

"A Difficult Stick" repeats a line after the title of Camille Dungy's "What I Know I Cannot Say."

"Fake Zombies" and "I'm Writing a Tornado" are found poems inspired by Naomi Shihab Nye's poem, "One Boy Told Me." They are the exact recorded words of Benjamin Bradshaw Frey and Josephine Clare Frey when they were ages 3–5.

"Upon Hearing the Animals One Mile into a Long Day's Drive Back to My PA Hometown" is after John Murillo's poem, "Upon Reading That Eric Dolphy Transcribed Even the Calls of Certain Species of Birds,."

Acknowledgements

My deep gratitude to the readers, editors, and journals who accepted the following pieces for publication:

Bellevue Literary Review	"Velcro Ode"
december magazine	"Danvers State Mental Hospital"
Live Encounters	"Grief"; "West Beach Again"; "To the Flour Handprints on My Wife's Pants"
New York Quarterly	"Chucks"; "My Sisters Paint My Dying Three-Year-Old's Nails"
One / Jacar Press	"Instructions for Deep Suction"
Passages North	"Hypothermia Part 2"
Tampa Review	"She Exits the Womb as Though on a Gurney"; "Night Nurses"; "Upon Hearing the Animals One Mile Into a Long Day's Drive Back to my PA Hometown"; "Mustard Seeds"

"A Difficult Stick," "The Pumping Room," and "Pink Feather Boa" won the 2023 Perkoff Prize for poetry at *The Missouri Review*.

A beginning list of gratitude:

I want to thank several extraordinary communities who gave such exquisite care to our daughter Charlotte and to us and who do the same for so many other children and families who need their skill and dedication: The therapists and specialists from Cape Ann Early Intervention, the doctors and nurses from CCS at Children's Hospital Boston, the doctors from North Shore Pediatrics, the doctors and nurses from PediPathways, and all of Charlotte's home nurses. Overwhelming gratitude as well to the therapists, social workers, volunteers, and incredible parents that form the community of The Perkins School for the Blind

Infant-Toddler program. And thank you to all of the doctors, social workers, and staff on the Pediatric Advanced Care Team at Dana Farber/Children's Hospital Boston who guided us through each day and phase of the final year of Charlotte's life, and then continued their guidance after her death.

Thank you to all of our friends, neighbors, and colleagues at Landmark School for your friendship and community and nonstop love and support. It was a gift to be with you and to be cared for by you over the years and especially during Charlotte's life and death and that first year after.

To the many people I haven't mentioned who played crucial roles in our lives and who inspired us and offered us help when we needed it, thank you. I hope to write many more pieces in honor of the friendship and care we received from so many of you, but of course, I will never really do it justice. So let me say, again, thank you.

Thank you to my writing guides, collaborators, and fellow sojourners: Dr. Suhail Hanna, Kirsten Bestor, Ryan Whitehouse, Janet Parady, Bill Flynn, and Derek Pierce. Thanks to the Feedback crew: Bill Chamberlain, Matt Schu, Erin Broudo, Jim and Jen Kuns, and Josh Broudo. Thanks to Catherine Reed for her encouragement and for founding the Walker's Zoom Writing Crew with Ben Barker, Carol Clark-Flanagan, Laurie MacAlpine, Eric Widmer, and Noël Grisanti. Thanks to Erin Ott and the Ada Limón draft-per-day crew. Thank you to Liss Couch-Edwards for her generous help with the cover. For their poems and for their support, I want to thank Naomi Shihab Nye, Tina Chang, Edgar Kunz, and David Rigsbee.

Thank you to the extraordinary students and faculty at The Ethel Walker School for your love and support and creative spirit.

Thank you to Wesley Kapp, Paul Corrigan, Jodi Johnson, Yuly Restrepo Garcés, Julie Nelson, and all the good folks at *Tampa Review* for your wonderful work, for believing in this book, and for bringing it out into the world.

A special thank you to Erin Broudo for sharing your time, your insights, your careful reading, and your encouragement. Thank you to Matt Blazer for your extraordinary partnership in writing retreats and endeavors. And thank you to Dave Thacker, whose thorough, demanding, brilliant, and heartfelt reading helped sculpt this book into what it is.

Thank you to all of our families, but especially Nicole, Andrew, and Maddie Ellrod, Erin and Michael Cartona, Kim Frey, Andrew and Sarah Frey. Thank you to Nick and Coreen Faraco for your utterly steadfast and persistent love and support. Thank you to my parents, Brad and Sue Frey—my first readers and teachers. Will, Ben, and Josie, I wish I could describe the honor and joy it is to be your dad. And Meryl, love, thank you for each step, *even to the edge*.

About the Author

Scott Frey grew up in Western Pennsylvania and teaches English at Pine Meadow Academy. He learned to teach and found his first writing community at The Landmark School. He then found a wonderful writers' community during his years teaching at The Ethel Walker School. He also served as a parent advisor for the Pediatric Advanced Care Team at Children's Hospital, Boston. He and his wife run a non-profit charity, The Charlotte Frey Foundation, whose mission is to help children with multiple handicaps and life-threatening illnesses improve their quality of life. Among other places, his work has been published in *Passages North*, *december magazine*, *One*, *Bellevue Literary Review*, and *The Missouri Review*, where he was awarded the 2023 Perkoff Prize for poetry. His prose chapbook, *Night Nurses*, was a winner in the 2023 Black River Chapbook Competition. He and his family live in Granby, Connecticut.

About the Book

Heavy Metal Nursing is set in Garamond Premier Pro digital fonts, based on original metal types by Claude Garamond and Robert Granjon that were designed and cast in Paris, France, in the sixteenth century. The book was designed and typeset by Wesley Kapp at the University of Tampa Press. The cover features photography by Liss Couch-Edward and was designed by Ana C. Alvarado Diaz.